BLOOD SISTERS OF THE REPUBLIC

Blood Sisters
of the
Republic

Poems by

Wendy Willis

Press 53
Winston-Salem

Press 53, LLC
PO Box 30314
Winston-Salem, NC 27130

First Edition

Copyright © 2012 by Wendy Willis

A Tom Lombardo Poetry Selection

Cover design by Kevin Morgan Watson

Cover art, "Tangled," by Patty Maher
Copyright © 2012 by Patty Maher,
used by permission of the artist.

Author photo by Christine Rucker
www.ChristineRucker.com

Printed on acid-free paper

ISBN 978-1-935708-64-3

for Ruby & Violet and all the sisters before them

and

for David

Acknowledgments

Many thanks to the editors of the following journals in which these poems first appeared:

The Alhambra Poetry Calendar: "Genealogy," "A House Divided"

Bellingham Review: "Oblation"

Burnside Review: "Speaking of Pyromancy or the Promise of Divination by Fire"

Clackamas Literary Review: "Sweet Blood"

The Legal Studies Forum: "Economies," "Thinking About Mary Baird Bryan Waiting for Her Husband To Return from the Oregon State Fair While I Wait for My Own New Husband To Come Home and the Republicans To Take Over the House of Representatives"

Phantom Kangaroo: "Seven Ways To Conjure the Luck of a Saltwater Sturgeon"

Poetry Northwest: "A Virtuous Wife"

VoiceCatcher: "The Marriage of Flax & Wool," "The Watering Hour Is Dark," "Violet at the Creation"

Windfall: "Native Species"

Zyzzyva: "The Half-Life of Strawberries," "The Second Half-Life of Strawberries"

CONTENTS

INTRODUCTION
by Tom Lombardo, Poetry Series Editor

When you read Robert Frost's poems, you know exactly where you are—in the woods of New England, steeped in irony and metaphor. When you read this inaugural collection from Wendy Willis, you'll know exactly where you are—in the rural Northwest, steeped in irony and metaphor.

In *Blood Sisters of the Republic*, Ms. Willis brings to life her deep roots along the green, rainy, fertile grounds of the Willamette and McKenzie Rivers and their tributaries in Lane County, Oregon. Today, this area borders the largest contiguous series of national parks that ride the Cascades and other mountain peaks from the Canadian border all the way south to Los Angeles, California.

These are the stories a mother passes along to her daughters, continuing the traditions passed to her through her Oregonian forebears. She offers them as a necessary sacrament of their young lives:

> *But since I am no longer a young woman, it seems a good time to come clean...*
> *I offer you this Eucharist.*
> *Take and eat.*

Ms. Willis' grandmother—one of seven sisters raised in rural Lane County, Oregon—learned the simple rules of life:

> *no crows in the house, dilute whiskey*
> *by half, clean fish downstream.*

From Ms. Willis' great-grandmother and her Bavarian Catholic forebears

> *she inherited*
> *their finely turned ankles and a gift*
> *for coaxing yeast.*

A pioneering matriarchy reverberates through the core of this collection, echoing the secrets of tough women locked into tough roles with few choices.

> *They gave her a rough-stitched apron…*
> *and a recipe for Christmas cake*
> *too rich for a woman to eat alone.*

There are weddings and funerals and meals to prepare and advice passed down from mother to daughter.

> *Which side of the family are you from?…*
> *The side that can keep a man?*
> *Or the one that can't?*
> *…*
> *we do not descend from beauty, but Visine & champagne*
> *can get us by.*

Willis' poems make frequent reference to the major economic engines of the pre-Nike Oregon—the agricultural lands bulging with fruits and berries like these strawberries…

> *The conical ones—Hoods and Northwest*
> *half shriveled pointed like nipples. Late honey sweet*
> *and too tender to travel.*

…and the products of the forest lands that cover the Oregon landscape in endless wilderness.

> *I was born under the sign of the pulp mill*
> *learned to love it long after owl wars*
> *shirred shut the shades.*

But the stories are told in what critic Harold Bloom would call authentic poetry, laden with figurations.

> *Dusk came*
> *down as a bruise, and silence,*
> *wide and black, laughed its secret laugh…*
> *…*
> *Because you say desire smells like corn*
> *and lure the yearling shadows close enough*
> *to nuzzle, we call you deer whisperer.*

Ms. Willis' *Blood Sisters of the Republic* offers not only her daughters but all of us a sensibility that respects place beyond our own existence, and maybe—hopefully—a connection to those who were here in the past and those of us who will be here in the future.

Economies of the 45th Parallel

THE HALF-LIFE OF STRAWBERRIES

Even old Mr. Cupp—should I say Farmer Cupp?—has plowed
them under now. The conical ones—Hoods & Northwests,
half-shriveled and pointed like nipples. Late-honey-sweet
and too tender to travel. Couldn't handle the truck trips.

Now thanks to the seedy-eyed botanists at universities
in California, the new farmers, the made-for-TV ones
with their dark-rimmed glasses and spit-creased overalls grow
Totems, Bentons, Shuksans, too. They're hardier, oblate—
at-the-ready for shiny Safeway tarts stacked with cardboard kiwi
and rock-hard peaches.

There's nobody on the old road now to pick anyway—well,
except for the spat-at mamas and daddies and their babies with fake
papers, fake dates of birth, sixteen by all typed accounts
but breastless and hairless and spilling over with fear,
with lies. But, before all that, back before the law and the plow, we'd hang

around—tight as baling wire—half-dancing and half-needing to pee,
waiting for the berry bus—mid-summer dusty & grinding gears—
soaked in desire, and I can't say now desire for who-knows-what,
but bleeding with it as a nimbus, as a halo.

By three o'clock, we—*we?*, you must ask. *We-who?* We, I mean,
we teenagers,
we hucksters. We who would become half-baked bakers and over-baked
lawyers and too-young mothers and more than that loggers, but loggers
who wouldn't last. That we. Those we. That's who I mean when
I say we—

overbrimmed, rancid with want, half-calved and bawling
for home but still remembering the morning dew on those low-down
plants, the ones St. Hildegard could not abide for their proximity
to snakes and other loamy things. But, that proximity, proxility,

prolixity, was the reason we'd shake off our teenaged throbbing,
our early morning thrum and return the next day
to our knees, and those loamy things
are the reason now, even now, I weep here—
in Mr. Cupp's old field
rimmed in over-oranged pumpkins and haunted by dust.

Economies

1.

I was born under the sign of the pulp mill.
Learned to love it long after owl wars
shirred shut the shades. Baby, I know onions
can keep up to six months, but I can't say what burns—
except tall grass & skinks. In this town,
false pregnancies are common among men.

2.

Answer me this: Should I measure my days
in un-ripe peaches and nail clippings? In screens
slamming or bees dropping?   There are field burns
& pandemics to consider.   And how do teacup
tempests stack up against the price of oil? In the end,
it's velocity that divides the sheep from the goats.

3.

Blueberries take two years to bear so I guess I'll kiss
the Catholic lawyer-poet direct on the lips.
But, at least it's April and the peas are in.
What powers the night light & the Ouija board?
Holy Mary, mother of God, crushing grapes, still
pink-lipped and blessed among women.

4.

A bird in the hand is worth two
in the bush unless the bush is burning
or the hand is grubbing or the bird
has learned to bite the hand
that feeds it (or the right
to remain silent).

5.

Is it beeswax or lye soap? Cattle futures
or cat calls? What then is the future
of the peach orchard or snow out of season?
What of the baby's nap or cradle cap?
Which storm gains & which shore loses?
What seeps? By that I mean, what hurts?

6.

I'm saving soup beans for the worst case,
but what do I know of loss? My daughters
can't tell time, and I neither admit nor deny
kissing lawyers. Or poets. Or skinks.
I avoided greenchain with skinny ankles
& a bird in the hand. Baby, open your ears now.

7.

Don't cook chicory in an iron pan.
It blacks. The sheik hangs men, but the state
of Oregon Arkansas West Virginia
Texas shoves a needle. I hear dandelion root
purges the liver. I wonder
if it works on hangmen or mules.

8.

My babies can't tell time, but this state's prisoners
are tinkering the clocks. A slave & a mule
are turned back on account of a false blue
warmspell. The border man sings:
Yes, sir. Yes, sir. Three bags full.
I'll give up maps for love.

9.

The eight-year-old's belly is tight as a button.
Cover your ears now. A book in the hand
is no different than sleeping timber rattlers
or half-hoarded auto bodies. False springs false
pregnancies false ceilings false confessions false
comparisons falsies. Baby, how can I tally that?

GENEALOGY

Maimed by plainness, adorned
only with adoration, she skittered—
avian and nervous—from a line
of robin-breasted sisters, hovering

between the old country and the frayed
edge of memory. She inherited
finely turned ankles, elaborate as spindles,
& a gift for coaxing yeast. Polishing

the edges of promises with dishtowels,
she practiced passing nickels
as secrets. Desire—a smooth
river rock—the rules were simple:

no crows in the house, dilute whiskey
by half, clean fish downstream.
They gave her a rough-stitched apron,
her name hidden in the seam

& a recipe for Christmas cake
too rich for a woman to eat alone.
She planned her wedding
for Chestnut Days. Dancing,

the balsamic moon. She wore
a girdle sown with sweetgrass
and nettle and made a vow,
jagged as a fishhook, *yes.*

The Marriage of Flax and Wool

A field of thick-fingered pickers pulls blue stalks and flails the bolls,
wailing one long note of blessing. Carding feathers from flax,
she curls her spindled legs, spinning inland on gristle and bone.

The betrothed arrives on time, his verse in straight lines—singing
jagged rocks and greening sun—while she turns the distaff as if
over the near-winter's ash can, the sky a pinhole just before splintering.

Each heartbeat, a fig blackens. Then she stands and keens
her tunneled silence, a burr in the mouth—smooth as oil—
the brown-blue orb of the iris. Even now, while the last light

licks at afternoon's arched neck and the goblets rest still,
she knows. The night's steady drip will not quench
the burning field with its milky blindness.

Native Species

for Ruby & for Violet

The rain on the wind called her children by name.
They were curled like acorns inside her,
smooth and waiting for a whiff of green
to coax them out. One day, they got too heavy

for her to carry alone. She lay on the black-green
bank and drank long, eyes sliding down
the sides of her head to keep watch
for speckled trout and the bright wing of osprey.

She opened her throat wide and round.
The rapids pushed in and flowed
through her skin onto the mossy ground.
The acorns cracked and two small girls dropped—

one by one—their roots curling around basalt
and fir, their branches reaching for sockeye
and filberts and huckleberries in season.
And, now, they know the wind's secret

names for beaver and salmonberry,
for great blue heron.

VIOLET AT THE CREATION

In April, before the clouds settled
their differences and the lake was still
nervous, she crawled into the garden
while a blue blackbird resembling nothing

more than a catfish sang arias
to give her cover. The apple-hipped
stepmother taught her a secret
game to fool the husband

who wore an egg-yolk jacket,
Dominion stitched in russet on the chest.
The pie-apple bride tossed
the little she high and her giggles

turned to pebbles dibblety dropped
until the husband raised an umbrella.
They tried on names like rumpled gowns.
Nanny goat called herself sloth

and humpback whale was torn
between winter wheat
and passenger pigeon.
Falcon christened himself

sapphire silence, blue jeweled
and unuttered, while she blew
spun glass through the straw
of her bones and plucked
her own name—Violet—from the new grass.

QUICKED

I can't but think of a sourdough start,
a packet of quick rising yeast,
the dance of vinegar & soda.
I can't but dream of oven-oranged
embers, the carmine heart of lithium.
Now, even this wan north sun melts the day
like a lozenge. I'll turn to the moon, I suppose,
a slick marble lodging in the throat.

REMITTANCES

after my grandmother, Edna

Granny, we're still afraid of snakes out here   on the edge.
I can't hear beetle wings slap   over the traffic,
and soon the windows will just be nailed   shut.

What do you want back from your fluttery
          letters?   I can tell you this:
The newscaster said swine flu
can cross borders. San Antonio's city fathers

have set traps.   Makes me wonder
about Phoenix & San Luis Obispo. Just learned
Oregon & Mexico   used to share a border.
That snake, the one I saw in Ireland with a baby on my back,

had legs. St. Patrick? I don't think so.   And the littlest one,
she's slipped   (a little) too. Chats in class.   Only one generation off
& not so afraid, while you sit at your kitchen table,
          all pressboard and creamed hominy.

You know—I'm a Catholic now, though no one speaks German
                                             here.
But it's all germane, and the Center for Disease Control
          has it down pat. The Mass is in English,
not that it matters

                              in that pursed congregation
of grapefruit juice and milk-white Jesus.   I pinched the pink foam rollers
and the egg timer with its   urgencies.

Is it Wednesday yet? When you get your hair set
and smoke your one cigarette out on the porch?
Margarine doesn't mean a damn thing anymore.
But marking time or split margins or blue flaming
                                        migraines   just   might.

Better bring back the butter churn.
The weather is mild and the President is   still

13

presidential. I had a good
haircut when he passed through

the tunnel. But no one asked me to predict   the next tide.
                    You know, I'm the one who can't remember
the names   of cousins to cousins,   the color
of rain after forest fire.   But, I can recall you sipping

pink wine with ice. Tonight my tongue is bitter
with remembering. In hell   they want ice water.
You're still as a sow bug and what is it
                    you want me to know?

That girls go and take the babies with them?
Do you wish I'd stayed back with the lazy boys
                    & dogs?
You didn't mention what I posited   about the tongue.

And you know what else?   Cassoulet is just hamburg
and macaroni. I can't keep track of   blackbirds
          or the names for rain. Here, you can see a dog run for three days.
What passes comes as butter and brown bread.

What did I forget
          to say? *The taste of the tongue is metal.*
Lovemaking requires a plinkety neck.
Did I forget to say: *Dogwood in high doses can be fatal.*

I'm looking for a little pink wine with ice,
but I'll have to settle for a cherry coke.   I didn't forget
about quick bread or freezer jam. I can still smell
          hazel sap on my hands, and I've hung

an extra five-gallon bucket   for wasps.
I'm just looking for a swimming hole and a sign.
                    Taxidermist: Restore faded mounts.
For snake bites, try Spanish fly & turpentine.

I'm not sure   the gods
know what to do with freshwater crabs or long hair.
Lice is for the poor of spirit,   and gravity
          has its own loyalties. This morning,

I couldn't remember the word for cardinal.   Only oriole
came to mind. So, I sang about you, the worms,
jink weed & Ovaltine.   Is the light still on?

Is the fridge stacked with coke and chicken & chokecherry pie?
          I can't stand that question about the chicken and the egg.
There's no debate.   It's the chicken.

Christ, what will I want when I'm the one
on the porch   and the nail counter comes
only once a week? I still can't decide: beggar,

baker, candlestick maker?   Now we understand each other.
It's worth a pinch —a catapult & a cold beer. You know,
A horse on her side
                    stands for a fool.

FIXED TIME

Wind riffles a child's skirt. Apples, too late
on the branch, flinch. A woman drops in the grass
to plunder hairpins & flicker eggs.
An old man on the bus checks his watch.
The wind kicks and a whistle drifts
up river. The Blues lives up to its name.
A thief flips a watch into his pocket. An old man
presses his lips to his wrist. A woman fiddles
a girl to school, both of them plum-eyed and licked.
A prisoner opens a clock shop and recalls
the feel of floor in every slick place. A warden
knows the feet's perils: *Shoes & socks required.*
A city is empty of clockmakers & cobblers,
weavers & haberdashers—prisoners assigned to tinker
and wind. A last priest keeps tick—this is the year
platters crack. Wind and child still riffle and chuff.
The old man slips. The woman sits. The flickers come back.
In the time it takes to split a lip, the apples go limp.

Herbert Hoover's Ghost Is the Fourteenth Guest

Bear with me awhile while I ask, what is it about the pear
that can tempt the saint to steal and an un-nerved orphan
to overindulge? I'm certain it's too simple to cite
the curves, even for an orphan. Or the Chinese certainty
the pear promises long life and good government.
No. Let me tell it to you straight—this one-horse state
can't afford to be choosy about its forbearers.

My daughters have taken to asking: How will your ghost smell? How? How, they ask,
how will we know when you've slipped into the room or lit on the seam of the bed?

You know, those girls' daddy still sings the original apologia
for Herbert Hoover, what with his rock-solid bearing & deep drawers
full of mining wares. And Augustine, stealing those pockmarked pears
insisted it was the company he was keeping. Some confessions.

The littlest girl asks: Can I wear your pink lace bra when you're dead? No matter my
granny's silverplate or the dog.

Herbert Hoover showed up in this state a chessplaying orphan and a ward
of Quakers. Spent his first hour in the pear orchard and his next
in the—how to put it delicately?—smallest room in the house.

My own granny's ghost smells of gentian violet & adding tape, of liver-spot cream
& telephone wire.

A chicken in every pot was a little far-fetched, but at least
Meatless Mondays stuck (it to the Catholics), and listen,
I'll stand with that hard-nosed Hoover on one thing—
a party for 13 will never do. Best have a stand-in
at the ready. Quoting himself: *Food will win the war.*

I'll be melted butter & bitter coffee or campfire smoke & late lilacs. Wet dog & wet ink.
First ramps & dandelion greens. I'd wish for a whiff of goat's milk & honey if those
darling girls wouldn't recognize me better from drug-store yarn & cheap champagne, but
for sure, something sweeter than a pocket copy of the Bill of Rights.

We're all asked to Hooverize now and then. To leave our blindspots
& a little blood spatter behind. It's good luck to cut your hair
on Good Friday. And Lou Hoover—from Waterloo—loving the locals
in her cotton gown, invited the brown people right in the front door.

The Hoover House—and the pear tree too—are now in the hands
of the Colonial Dames. Old Hoover's ghost is left to reign
over hobo camps & empty mines, over late autumn ashcans,
over bankers and breadlines, over banquets for thirteen.

*And, ah, those little girls sleeping still wait for the creak of the crooked floor. They
wait for hard-soled boots brushed against the door & a still-warm haunch perched
on the seam of the bed. They still wait for the milk-hot breath, for the half-lit kiss.*

Humming the Householder's Hymn

QUICKED

Yes, then, let it in.
The wind fired with sand,
let it in. The tortoise, rutting
at midnight, in! And the cockroach
in the half-drunk wine glass,
let it in! The scorpion,
the packer, in. Let them in!
The jungle, the creeping
nightshade. In. In.
And the Mayans, fierce
but never tall enough,
let them in, too.
The bitter coffee with cream—
in & in. A piggin full,
a porridge pot, a pipkin,
a spittoon then, let's go with that.
In. Too rough for an amphora,
not a beaker or a flask.
Oh! Drawer or gunny sack,
pitcher or velvet pouch,
a trough or a trinket box,
barrel or breadbox? In!
Yes, mailpouch and mixing bowl,
teacup, thimble, cog.
The flask screws too tight.
A file is too flat.
But, powderbox, pill box,
reliquary, spoon. In.
The washbasin
the general piled his mail in.
A cask, a birdbath,
a kitbag, a flowerpot, a trough.
Hamper and laundry basket,
chifferobe,
bed pan,
scuttle for coal.

Hark box & salt box.
Trunk.
Credenza.
Hutch.

A monstrance, a votive, a censer,
a wineskin filled with smoke
for I am his love
& I let him in.

OBLATION

I offer you my hands—bony and blue-veined,
brittle but skilled at stitches and picking tiny
beads from polished wood floors. But maybe
you need broad palms blistered and rough
from an honest day's work.

I offer you sugary confections made at midnight
from coconut stashed in hidden cupboards,
spiked with Frangelico. But maybe
it's steak you crave—bloody & dense,
smelling still of prairie grass and dust.

I offer you my tangled hair—a veil
entwined with birds' nests and tales
of the inky night. But maybe
you lean toward the day—shorn
& gleaming & featherless.

I offer you this Eucharist.
Take and eat. But you,
a bored congregant, devour
the host without lingering
over a moment of flesh.

THE WATERING HOUR IS DARK

Words are altered
Rather than destroyed
—Democritus

The grass grows ragged and sunflowers languish,
the summer of the year of ones—the anniversary
season of thistles and lies. Bees slink back and tat
fennel from seed to lattice, and slurry lettuce
disturbs a sow bug's gray sleep. Meet
that blue-bobbed hour before the sky rips
like cheesecloth; we'll ignore the voice
of the walking God—not falling for the tinny
imitation of a high season chick-a-dee-dee-dee.
You'll lean a hoe slanting south, uncompassed
in devotion and sow into a dandelion's heart.
Now, the watering hour is dark and the air sweet
with rot. I trace the name of the blue-eyed mother
in weevily flour and sew aprons, leaf upon leaf.
You set the lock against the cantor's psalm,
ringing like a toothache. Nothing's left but bruised
plums over the fence and prayers
molting for an hour's ungraveled sleep.

Fruitcake Weather

The day shattered early for glazed
cherries and too warm by half
to season the wedding whisk
or seek citron in the stacks. She settled
on Sultanas & drug store brandy
& an apron from under the porch.

> The candidate with his mechanical arm
> passed,
> blowing sand into glass,
> sloughing for a prophet.

A smidgen, she said, that means a pinch
and a pinch is what you hold
between your thumb and index finger.

Under a hogkilling sky, she prayed
for the luck of rain, for an unseasoned
squall. For a talon's clutch of sugar.
For 4 & 20 blackbirds.
There is fortune in the building of a woodpile.

> The old man selling scuppernongs said:
> *War is close at hand.*
> He stooped and spilled
> his bee-hive globes

while her lips spread to splitting.
Her daddy always said: *Grab a root and growl.*

She didn't wait for dainties
or a shivaree moon,
just white sauce with lumps,
and a pantry matron with a limp.
The pond truck was full of fish heads
and the driver sang for the next best thing.

This is the first time asking
called the man spinning yarn
from the rabbit
in his lap.

On the 20th, timber rattlers moved
to their winter dens. She scooped
pineapple dropped from a ship
and figs planted in fealty
to some inside-out nation.

A waxpaper bride with a heart
of make-do, she filled the pan
with treacle and sorghum snatched
from under a widow's window.
Wrap in a cloth moistened with brandy.

A Fleet wedding in the end,
though the courthouse carried
its own latitude. 36 degrees,
North. The men circled
and softened in their cells,
the women sharpened their guilt.

What haunts us here?
What blood?
What blast?
What hung?

Without the tinny call
of the last banns
the day rolled open like parchment
and the linnet was silent
for a note. Just a barbed stutter
before she quilled a nest
for copper and eggs,
before she riffled the shades
and breathed: *I will.*

A Virtuous Wife

There was no overture for her short walk
A cloud of crows cried: *come,*
come, dropping the *ai* in maiden,
 and declaiming the sky, frail

as a robin's shell, cracking its late blue
promise of glittering yolk. Dusk came
brown as a bruise, and silence—
wide and black—laughed its secret laugh.

Summer's flames burned early, out of season.
With musky devotion, she lit her hands
on the loom & slipped her shawl,
stirring the sleeping God with a glint
of tobacco-freckled clavicle.

Even the daughters with their honed
sweetness asked: *How did you?,*
crooning birdlike and green as the bottom
of the river, and the old dog—
disguised as a sheep—fooled

the west wind with his rusty smell
and fealty to the one long-needled pine.
The smallest, with her spine
fanned as a hidden fern,

leaned into winter and said *I can smell you*
here like apples, like sugared apples
and nighthawks whistled
their one thought: *now.*

A House Divided

There'll be wine jelly for Appomattox Day
so long as I stay on my feet and the weather
holds. But the wind's turned cold
and all my promises have been cashed in.
Surely, the rain's close behind now.

Last night, the dog dawdled out at midnight,
and the neighbors, they danced. They danced!
She with her sweet-pickle voice and blunt-cut
fringe. He with his spoon-faced shuffle
and flash of dying, oyster-slick thigh.

But last night, last night when the moon was high,
they were yellowed sweet by the lampshade
and the dusty curtain. Is that what it takes
to keep the troth? We could never dance like that—
half-drunk and forgetting the wind. Even the late geese

can't sashay up to speed now. Only once,
that April night, the one when the mayor
sang, we stumbled close, your slingshot
arm wrapping me in, both of us knowing
my faithless horse was already in the yard.

I dreamed I couldn't find you in the cellar,
and the old dog died in my arms.
You know, the Yankee general showed up
at the courthouse in his field blues,
muddy and shame-faced over his height.

The concords are dusky, on edge,
and for certain won't keep til spring.
I can't help but pass the hat.
The lonely mayor. The wavery tenor.
Rain pouring out of the eaves.

April'll come again and we'll still
be wondering about winners
and losers. But, it wasn't really a fair
fight, now, was it? Wrap. Unwrap.
Wrap. Oh! What man can put asunder.

SWEET BLOOD

for Ruby

Because you say desire smells like corn
and lure the yearling shadows close enough
to nuzzle, we call you deer whisperer.

Because you hiccup as the incense
ball nears, we pour salt
in the furthest corner of the yard.

Because you whisper the hummingbird's secrets,
we learn to split the baby & glue splinters
back to bark. For those graces, you'll pay

in cinnamon and cabbages. And though I don't recall
whose arms I abandoned as you mewled
at the old maid's wedding,

it was not a single-grained silence
shattered but an invocation
of mermaid hair and green glass baubles.

Because I hold you in my hand—a watermelon seed,
an amulet against late summer's backward glances,
you can not be passed one apron to the next.

Your just-finished skin, thin as grapeskin,
drapes your sweet blood as your father and I glance
one last time. I cry your name in a gasp.

Easter Eggs for Ruby

*

Girl, it's been a good long while since I sang for the dead.
I sniff the wind for a sign but fall asleep like a heretic
or a prophet—a donkey at my feet. Dream of brining
pickles, tomatoes rotting on the vine. The freighter lists
slow enough here, and I'm afraid to go on.
But I can say this: *Buffle-headed ducks will eat molasses.*

*

Rains all day then hails. Hard. You search for eggs at dusk,
still wearing your Christmas dress, tight across the middle.
If we're lucky, hot cross buns will keep for May Day
or a wayward whim. You're all new curves and fear of pain.
Hike your skirt for the host. *Amen.* Too cold even for frogs.
I don't know how to trap eels. I don't want you to either.

*

In the year of the frog, we'll prime the kettle
to track the planets. Dimpled as a dumpling,
don't forget your pocketbook or a lock of the dead dog's hair.
A startled cow and a nervous milker do not go well.
When I say eclipse, I mean daddy. When I say stop,
do. You: *Mama, can I weave this trap when you're dead?*

*

I'm praying you find frog eggs with their jelly promises
and elver cake. Dumpling monkey doughy darling girl,
I want to squirrel something beautiful, bury it
in the backyard, to show you the rabbit in the Renwick,
with its come hither hither and circlety fear.
Remember: *Bees swarm the quarrelsome.*

*

It's true. When I say apple core, I mean heartbreak.
When I say leftover, I mean blind woman, I mean
headache & biscuit recipe & jelly jar,
the zipped breath of a car start, a train-whistle promise.
My biscuit, my crumpet, my dumpling,
when I say milk, I mean walk slow.

*

If asked, I'll tell you when to open the drapes.
When to cricket them shut and when to rip
stitches from the wall. Don't sleep too long
in the sun. Put down the basketball.
Take the June bug in your mouth.
Rip.

*

The blue ship turns. *Ahoy!* Incanting thunderish clouds,
you know the compass down to the quarter turn
but can't keep track of hours. Never mind minutes
or inches. Coppice the ash! It smells of wet dog
and selfishness. It'll be eel pie & mash
& ketchup from daddy. Darling, dumplings are easy.

*

The window presses out on the alley wondering
what hour is it? Did we forget your daddy's birthday?
Maybe it's winter's lingering that rattles and nerves,
the closeness of the kitchen that makes us miss
God's hot breath, rancid and jittery as a June bug.
Velocity may crush us both. Lean in now. Close.

*

The cherry tree has started its party. The potatoes
have eyes and the maid is salmoning the broom.
There's this, too: We Catholics don't know the first thing
about Beatitudes or tide tables. Now it's all
long red hair & Wyoming. Dumpling darling,
adore your daddy? I used to be better at this.

*

Even the dead need a wash and set. And you?
You need a once-over, too. Meet me in your nightgown,
the one with the rough lace. Tell me what it means to dream
of a pollywog. Maybe then I'll remember how
to tenderize the heart, to make chicken & dumplings.
Maybe my pie crusts won't be caraway-clouded, clinging.

*

It's harder yet to know what to love—lemonade,
the ironing board or butter? The coiled black of black?
And still, you blue-blame the wrists for sniggling
an eel with a lob worm. At least it's a fairer fight.
Burnt honey & yeast, curvy as a question mark,
I've never even seen a Caribou. How can you believe a word?

*

When I say Laplander or fire-in-the-hole or greasy spoon,
I mean blind alley. I mean heartworm. I mean
girl oh girl oh girl. David told you: *In Texas,
only the belt-buckles are beautiful.* I say eel
& dumpling & frog. I mean stop. Buffle close.
Ah girl, at least the tongue teaches itself.

VIOLET'S KITE

We choose the cheap one
with the pony you call Pinky Pie
or sometimes Cupcake.
You hop on one foot.
      Up. Fast in the first tick. Then run.
The kite rips from the string and dishes
into the whippy grass.

Stickless and wounded,
it jinks and skirrs.
You run and run to zibble it up,
face turned to the pearled-off sky.
You're frog-blind and fast.
I can't hear your song in the wind.

2.

You tell the old man you want to be a farmer. He says: *Hail!*
    Then,
    you pinch a lipstick from my purse and move on.
I can't recall the details, the cat & mouse tales, Violet. But I recognize
    the tiny pick pick pick
    of my grandmother's walk—
    you do it on a high wall and disguise
the zinc-white paper of her skin.
Don't listen too close. There'll be hours enough to nitter
    about the blue dance
    & the black dress
    & keeping your nails short.
There'll be time to explicate yield signs
    & dry measures & prophylactics.
Don't look away. I know about the egg in your mouth
& the grapes & stolen gelt
you ate behind my sour bed.

3.

Which side of the family are you from?

The inside or the outside
    The pie side or the cake side
        The poker side or the bridge side
            The fat side or the skinny side
                The horse side or the dragon side
                    The garden side or the cook side
                        The minstrel side or the gypsy side?

Which side, child?
The side that can keep a man?
                Or the one that can't?

4.

There's cherry pie left over in the fridge and a few things must be said:

> We do not descend from beauty, honey, but Visine & champagne
> > can get us by.
> My mother never wore a crucifix to bed
> > & dogs
> > were to sleep on the porch.
> Our feet get wider with age but at least the arch is high
> > and our ankles are fine.
> Grandma Edna hid her ashtray in the oven. Mine's
> under the back porch.
> > Just two cigarettes.
> > After the dishes are done.

> Snack on canned pears and cottage cheese while your lover naps.
> With your blue-cold lips, you can nip jelly fish and kiss peppers.
> The April moons are these: pink moon, sprouting grass moon,
> > fish moon, egg moon.
> It's never too early to understand what happens
> > between hot water and yeast.

That's enough, then. Please forgive my vinegary breath.

5.

Child, beetle closer here in the dark. It'll be Easter Monday
soon enough and a Spring tide, too. I wish
I could show you the Delaware blue eggs
and the bleeding edge of rimrock. I'd rub you
between my fingers to smooth the edges,
but I love the skidmarks too hard.

6.

Oh, hold it here, with your patchwork skin and pink moon mind.
Hold it here, the frog's eggs and half-dollars in your pockets.
And that shimmery hipped dance, hold it.
Hold it here—close—your blue lips and pelt of sleep.
Crown the lunch hour, the make do, the peanut butter &
        boiled eggs tough as horsehide.
Oh hold it with your seawater stink and sticky rose tongue.
        Hold it here. Hold it hold it. Here.

It's only lunch. It's only the wind. It's only one lost dance.
It's only a jelly fish. It's only the moon. Violet, Violet. It's only a kite.

Dear Dumpling

There's talk of warships in the harbor

Giving me hopes for slipping gossipy lips
From our so nearly licit love, my love.
Skirted ships—patched pink—in the Kaiser Yards.
But, my duck, in well-regulated households,
They remove gum with gasoline.
They don't confuse a toothpick
With a pickaxe.   And, even now, I ache
To set tack. Your courtesan yet,
I still souse apple tea for the sick.
It's not even nightfall, and I'll sing like clockwork.
Packing in piano and pram. You know
Today, we picnicked in the purlieu,
And I was still jealous of the jackrabbit.
Me (with my lovelock) cuckolded he (with his VanDyke).
It was a shortsell on startle. The milk is already spilt,
And I'm hooked—sloe-eyed and blowzy,
Poisoned by buckthorn. Laid askance,
Wondering *what happened to the whisk?*

Pepper makes my leg ache,

But, in this age, pigeon,
There's no excuse
For dalliances or rancidity.
But the suet's gone off
And even the chickadees
—With their black caps—
Keep their distance.
Decamp the poplars,
With the prunes laid up
And prudery just packed.
Before the paint is dry—
Decamp the poplars.
Abandon the whisk.
Race the glitter for the bridge.
Lackaday, lo and behold,
You *can* kill a fly with milk.

I never could stand lettuce

But it's tolerable now, hot and buttered.
The neighbor, back-combed and crimped,
Called a great horned from the eaves.
It looped left, hellbound for Arkansas.
Chickabiddy, you'll arrive not a moment
Too soon, and the figs already half-rotted.
Arc and saw, sweet fiddle and shell,
You're a long ways out yet.
I still can't find the whisk.
I'll filch dram and noggin
So there'll be cherry bounce
And a lime in waxed paper
For Christmas. Candle the eggs.
Bundle the yolks. Don't coddle
The night gnats. Spirits of camphor
Will whisp them along and sprinkle
A thimbleful of sense on the children.

Oh, now the dog's gone sweet

And is layed in for the night.
Can find no use chasing raccoons
Down the mew with its chuckholes
And garlic-lorn ghosts. Griddlecakes,
Christmas is over & we should be shacked
Up by now. Already slow-soaking
The black-eyed peas. You know,
A well-regulated household has Jaffe water
Ready to scare the linens white.
But here, we're stuck. It's a biddy hen, a brick,
A cackle come too late.
While the neighbors hector their bunkus
Over the back, I'll let the garden rot
'Til its time to wheedle the wheelbarrow.
Where is the whisk?
The children sit tight. Knife off the cream.
By now, they're frocked and half-clacked.

*

We have no socks

The children champ and chirp
Do you suppose they suffer then,
Sockless and bunked in? Mincemeat-
And-milk, the little one's finally in the pink,
But the big one's box-eyed and flecked.
A great yoke, for sure. Though the garden's
Gone gritty, my fingers still click.
I'll just break the skein
To start again. I'll skirt the frayed
Territory to starch and pin up
The flank. You know, there's onion
Tonic for thin hair. Will you call
Just to call it a fluke?
It's too late to cant now.
Knock-kneed and adored,
I'll ask you one last time:
How does the clock work?

House Finch Returns To Chastise the Household for Its Late Winter Lassitude

We know by now that children no longer learn
cursive. They loop along fine with *sans serif* and Vs
broken free from their Es. It's a topic for a *tsk tsk*, a chance
to recall *our hallowed days*. Who—we ask—will decipher
the missives of poets and philosopher kings?
Meanwhile that chirripity bird, with its heart
stained on its breast, has its own set of opinions.
But I'm not sure they're worth a Continental.
It's all-out racket, an unplanned tell-it-to-
me-brother-Amen. I know it's bunk
but I can't help but think twice
about girls budding breasts too early
and boys bedding down in the desert.
Why of all the unholy households in this Republic
did it choose this one to chastise? Is there so much
to mistrust because last fall's caterpillars
still curl in the jelly jar? Because we can't call
our ghosts by name? There must be legions of them:
fishermen & lumbermen & lonely women.
For our defense we've settled on this:
It's a force majeure. A planquer.
The certitude of wars that won't end.
We've given ourselves over to sugar ants
& mid-afternoon champagne. The furrows are fallow.
We may as well beat prams into ploughshares now
with the President and his milk-skinned men
coiled at the ready while our one curvy girl
curling on my lap but too big to fully fit,
twists—cruelly—the tails of Gs and Ys
practicing for roll call & roadhouses & roles
we have yet to name. Ah Spring!, fine bird,
surely can't be that far off now for I am fretting
about the long-legged nature of things,
tilting one pink ear for answers, disinclined to go on.

PROVIDENCES

SEVEN WAYS TO CONJURE THE LUCK
OF A SALTWATER STURGEON

1. We are obliged to seek forgiveness
from darkling ghosts for the backwaters of
what we thought we thought. 2. Beware a road
pitted with milkweed and vinca for surely
it ends in an opaque city, a squared-
off mayor & *missus can you spare some*
change? 3. Four white feet are unlucky on
a racing pony. Never bet on a
gray. 4. Drink deep a cup cured by forest
fire & late rain. 5. You can't warm to the
title *widow* without kissing its round-
O mouth and carrying home a scrap-purse
of stones. 6. Press slow toward the milk-sotted
morning for fear of sparrows and slant-dreams.
7. Set the hook. Spit on the worm for luck.

How It Came To Be That the Rook Took the Queen

for my father

You know, I never did see a coyote in town.
Though I kept suggesting so, spinning tales
of link-gold eyes, a lowdown slink to distract
from the fact that I could not track how the rook's
straight path could end in a hook or how to calculate
the area East of a hypotenuse. No.
And I still do not know how to add by abacus
though I brought you one on more than one occasion.

But since I am no longer a young woman, it seems a good time
to come clean: I did see a horse in a green velvet jacket
& an executioner's eyeshade. A clamour of rooks
on the grounds of the Tower of London. And, in New York City,
they've got an aircraft carrier for show. But, why didn't I tell you
about that? About the blanched branches of the curly willow
and the sky dimmed half-dark and pink? And, why
didn't I tell you about when the cherry tree out front split

in two? That tree was fruit-barren but showy so it was as pink
as it would ever be. The March rains kept on and it fell—
bustle up—like a fancy woman in a parade. Why, then,
didn't I tell you that? In the midst of all that saying
and not, still you shimmied up the ladder, father,
oh father, knuckles creaking and pointing north, knees clanking
against the garage, you shoveled the gutters. Even then, did you know
of the one hundred bulls Pythagoras ordered slaughtered

in honor of the theorem while I was down there holding the ladder
and holding forth about the dreamed-up coyote bedding down
in the peonies and slipping the Thanksgiving carcass
off the porch? Did you know that he—Pythagoras,
not the coyote—was reputed to have a golden thigh?
I know you know it's bad luck to hang a calendar
before January the first, to light three cigarettes
on one match, to plant seeds in the last four days

of March. And you'll recall that Judas Iscariot
was the thirteenth banquet guest. For that, Herbert Hoover
wouldn't tolerate dinner for one more than twelve. No,
they hired a stand-in. Father, you goodly mathematician,
do you believe me when I tell you I never knew til now
that *squared* as in three squared is nine as in four squared
is sixteen as in a-squared plus b-squared meant a thing?

No.

But, slowly now, the rooks (and you) are gone silent in this frayed
afternoon light & I can see the roof's pitched peaks casting off shadows.
Squares. Ah, squared. As in nailed together four-sided, solid-square.
And suddenly Pythagoras & his smoky bulls & his prohibition
against the eating of meat & even beans & the shimmer off the roof
& the use of the abacus to teach math to the blind, it all comes together.
And I can see the chess-rook make a hooked move toward the queen
and a ladder leaning south is most certainly a sign of love.

Thinking About Mary Baird Bryan Waiting for Her Husband To Return From the Oregon State Fair While I Wait for My Own New Husband To Come Home and the Republicans To Take Over the House of Representatives

Labor Day and the bluebottles must have been thick
even still—glittery clouds feasting on high-peak corn

and nipping at the nether regions of horses
and Presbyterians. I'm certain the baby's dress

drooped and red-ringed her neck in that late heat,
while your stemwound husband took the train

to the provinces to moralize about the evils
of the gold standard and the virtues of local wool.

And here I sit listening to the round thump of a moth
against the window, half rooting for it to crack

glass and half wondering about the cruelty
of things. I'm crampy and early-cold and down deep

know my womb is hollow for good. With my first big girl,
my water broke on the way to court. I was a lawyer married

to a lawyer then, too, sister, but I had the good sense
to see where that was headed. I'm trying to stay focused

but the bottom drops out thinking about those back-combed
hucksters headed for the House fueled by corn subsidies and lies

and about you, rocking the empty cradle with your foot
and knitting in high-sermon iambs, your fine mind singeing

over the price of gold and the fate of the pauper.
I'll bet you've painted your desk red and the children are haloed

with dust and heat. Remember your first baby? Lanky now
and half-budded, but back then you could not stop bead-counting

her toes like a Papist. You coo-cooed her downy fur and even you
couldn't help but sing "monkey" into her teacup ear.   Her feet won't fit

in your hands now, but she is a fast-talking force headed for Congress.
Blessed are the meek, Mary, and insanity is an imperfect defense.

My bed's empty, too, while my husband sleeps in a sloped room
in a sloped bed in a state sloping toward the sea. You understand.

He's got upstanding business on the road.   But, Mary, you shouldn't worry
too much about the fair. That state fair is full of potluck ladies,

short-veiled hats & Methodist farmers. They don't allow
hypnotists. Even on the side where the barkers are toothless

& sway an oily spell—snake charmers all—the sensualists are few.
I'm certain you wouldn't approve of the ropers nipping the kegs

behind the sheep barn and I don't know for sure where you fall
on horse racing, but you'll get some fine blankets for your trouble.

Mary Baird Bryan, wife and braintrust of Platte populism,
Mary Baird Bryan, lawyer and standard bearer of flat-land justice,

Mary Baird Bryan, speech-writer and Nebraska breather of fire,
Mary Baird Jennings Bryan, I hate to be the one to tell you what's going on

in Lincoln now. That seat you earned by polishing virtue, spit-shining
forthrightness, is under the road-worn rump of a Republican

& a Catholic to boot. He's slipped on your man's mantle & a blue-white
smile dripping a tinny *we-the-people*, promising a haul of commodity cheese.

Half-drawled populism is nowhere near what it used to be.
It's all big banks and soy futures now and both of us knitting booties

in the near-dark worrying about our bona fides. Both of us worrying
on the future of the Republic and the charms of casseroles and half-veils.

Both of us worrying the babies we had and touching one cold
thimble-worn finger to the ones we didn't. Both of us swallowing

the dark just before the sky turns to the next shade of mud.
Both of us, Mary, listening for the whistle of the train off the river.

The Second Half-Life of Strawberries

Listen, there's no consolation for a misconception or a miscarriage
or even a fussy stomach on a long night. But strawberries—
in their scarlet perfection—make a credible cure for gout.
My bowl runneth over.   I hear that the oblate King's
second wife or half-wife or second half-of-life-wife,
she didn't have a chance, what with her tiny neck
and her third nipple, the one—they say—that was for suckling the devil.
A strawberry mark, a port-wine stain, a goiter, a mole.

A mole:

a small velvety-furred burrowing mammal having small eyes and fossorial forefeet.

She may have had eleven fingers, too—Queen Anne—though it's hard
to say for certain what with all those bell sleeves and velvety lies. She always
had a bun in the oven but the boys didn't stick. Even with the supplication,
the fussed-over ovaries & tin pan ovations – still the same overtures
swirling around her tiny neck, with a strawberry to mark the spot.
But even so, she was said to have been charming with her perfect French.
I hear that the French word for desire is *envie*, and I know what they mean.
It's a make-do world, and I'll take my envy soaked in cream.

A mole:

a fleshy abnormal mass formed in the uterus by the degeneration of an ovum.

You know, the strawberry is never even mentioned
in the Bible, though I know it does a world of whitening
for the teeth & skin. The eunuchs carved them in cathedrals,
and French ladies macerated them in the bath.
The Virgin Mary picks strawberries each St. John's Day,
and April has a strawberry moon though they come on in June.
And listen, that skinny-necked queen, she should have known:
never split a double berry for fear of love (and the king).

A mole:

a spy who works from within the ranks of an enemy.

In the end, I guess the king—reeking of the clap—took pity on his wife,
calling up France's best headsmen, having swords sharpened special.
It was a pity, for sure, depriving the guillotine and it's slab-handed
peasant of that spindly neck, of that strawberry stork's mark,
of that saucer-white throat. For now, I've lost my appetite.
Let the berries rot. Let them rot like half-forgot roses,
turned to vinegar in their blueing bowl, bloody and soft and still sweet.

AND IT APPEARS THAT—ONCE AGAIN—ALL THE BLUES ARE ON HAND

After Portrait of Postman Roulin,
Vincent Van Gogh
Detroit Institute of Art

But now, I spend my time searching for a wisp
out of reach, for even serviceable French,
for *enchanté & desolé.* For a moment stamped
here & now. What is it about the mind made visible
in the cracked cornflower wall? It's a tell,
Monsieur R, you could be a sea captain
but for your bead-blue eyes, not horizon-weary
but nearsighted and sparking for a brindle-back.

Sixty percent will say their favorite color
is blue. I wonder. Is it for blueberries
or baby powder, a sky-sick Navy or love
for the Saxton sea? Is it for a grandmother's
gentian or latent loyalty to Napoleon or the steel
of the last century? Half-buried porcelain
or just an empty palm to declare a milk-sotted truce?
I wonder. Could I have been a sea captain

but for *mal de mer* & bald-faced failures with a compass
& two psychics who raised the flag of drowning?
You could be a police officer gatekeeper jail keeper key
keeper, keeper of the peace. Zookeeper? Maybe.
But not anything close to a stable keeper or a bar keep—
you must be something requiring the I-mean-business blue
of the state (or its proxies). For me, it's an outright search for nouns.

The neighbors called Van Gogh *Fou Rou* for a reason—
all that *mal de tête* in the fierce night sky.
My littlest little girl: *what does it feel like to be a fish?*
I reply: *wet.* But, I can't say: *the mind splinters*
& insists you could have been an astronaut.
(But what of airsickness and vertigo
and grief for the spinning blue planet?)

I could recall the sea blue wall if only the sea
were such a color, rendered by a foreigner, a mad man, a maker
of the blue of nations the blue of warhawks and love, doves.
The blue of oblivion. Of the mind peeling off in gritty, lethal flakes.
I could have been a clam digger. You, a conductor, a chancellor.
A postman is better anyway. Amongst splintered women
& salty dogs. Ah, *Sacré Bleu!* you can smell the mind
run amok. You can hear it smoke.

Blessed are the bored & brindled. The lovelorn
& the seasick. Blessed are the stern & right,
the silvered & the split. The iced-in stars, the warhawks,
the doves. *En Francais: beni.* Blessed is the smoke.
Blessed is the fire and last cold spark.
Blessed are the blustering & the brackish.
Blessed is the forgetting.
Beni soit l'oubli. Beni soit le bleu.
Blessed is the blue.

WRITING HOME FROM ALABAMA ON THE ANNIVERSARY OF
ASKING *WHAT IS IT THAT ATTRACTS YOU PERSONALLY TO
THE CROW?* THEN PASSING TED HUGHES FROM HAND TO
HAND IN ALL HIS BLOODINESS

You don't have to say. I know this is a letter long overdue,
but why should we owl away our celebrating hours
tallying loss?   And, I know. I forgot to mention
the china doll dug up from our garden,
late season straw for hair and forced-open eyes.
Crippled by early slugs and squirreled away now
a good long time in a hung-up pocket. But, my love,
I just know. It's the mulishness that shatters the glamour.

Some days—like the one we met—should be marked
on the calendar with blue chalk and glitter, but instead
that night started with a full-faced moon, basted taut
to puckering like you could unravel it with one good pull,
lure it down close with a glass of milk and a shot
of Southern Comfort. But maybe it just needed
a seat, a haberdasher, a slice of brown sugar pie.

I spent all the days up to that one trying to stick North
of the Mason Dixon. Then how'd I find myself on a rickety train
with dog-eared Hughes and a ticket to Alabama?
It's all gentiles down here in Point Clear. The kudzu leans
the barns and the oil rigs leak shimmery. Thank God for Mississippi.
The last time we sat down side-by-side was way back on St. Eulalia's Day.

I suppose you must recall when I tried to seduce you
with an orange. A wounded one, warted and bitter
laid across my palm.   Looking back, I wish I'd used a persimmon—
one of those glowing ones from the churchyard
that can outlast the first frost but are always done in
by the second. When a cardinal appears, it's time to turn back.

My handwriting's gone feral & I'm certain I can feel
the laundry piling up resentments. I know enough now
to say we both need long light and leisurely sky.
But still I want to tuck in the brush and wait
to see the stag leap. I invited the black dog in.
And that I regret. This year, we'll try again for profiteroles.
Surely we're over winter's hump now and the Easter Lilies'll

be led out by the grocer.   On the train, the couple behind me
is flirting over a fugue. Her English is chittery. He taps
the back of my seat. Is it an omen? Like dreaming of an eclipse?
They're sparring over the virtues of the electric organ. He's found
Jesus. She's lapsed.   Darling, this planet'll wear us out
yet and we'll be left to spin nettle cloth from memory.

The lady in the supper line reminded you to keep a woman
who can throw flour on the counter for buns. And you know
I know the price for a boxwood spindle is a dozen eggs.
When it's evening over Mobile Bay—right there
where the Tecumseh sunk—the pelicans loop the downdraft
like a tracing wheel on onion paper. Long and loped
and brutal. I admit it. The doll's skull is cracked.

The clouds are late lilacs, and there's a path
pounded down to the lake. But you know,
I can dog my way home now. I can recall the hour
you taught me about the saucer that cools the cup,
to use the word thicket in a sentence, to swallow
a laugh by sucking a sugar cube. Like you say
we've always got the order wrong.   This is a letter long overdue.

A FRESH ARGUMENT WITH FORMER FRIENDS AGAINST UNFETTERED FAITH IN PULLING TRUMP FIRST

They say the devil stitches round the edges of tables
where cards are played. *Wear a hat to keep him at bay.*
Well, that's advice I can heed, but I'm missing that devil
now, bless his spady heart. He's slipped through the cracks
since I packed it in and pulled down my starched cap.

Looking back, I think I failed to warn: *Don't play bridge
with a cross-eyed man.* But, I can't figure which hand
landed before I was laid flat. It wasn't the slipshod
vows finally shed so much as the cake's slip & fall.
Nobody died after all. Sure, I wrote out a funeral

like some fevered wish, but you know, even then—
champagne-lit and going for broke, the old lady's ghost
creaked the floor and called for hearts. I know.
Back then I flirted the devil with my bare head
and invited in the truculent. But there's no suspense:

I ended teakettle up by the back door. Since then,
hardly a word's passed between us, but you'll be pleased
to hear you can play cards in public in the old colonies now.
Or at least at pubs in Wilmington where everyone's
looking the other way in favor of the Stanley Cup.

There are hatless men there—right out front—
pulling what they can with their whatnot, singing
sloshy songs and holding their ears, splitting
pairs over Canada beers, splitting their time
between the body check and the quick trick.

They make me wish I'd been better at the barbed blow
instead of wasting time ginning up tea cups
spilling over with tawny port and zipped up gin
and tonics. I felt like a force to face back then,
but I just held diamonds, headachy and chipped.

You, you fickle friends. I know. The four of clubs
is the devil's four-poster bed. I tried to tell you: *It's unlucky*
to pass a beggar without tossing a token. Call for trump
with knocked knuckles. Drop a red card for luck.
I even fed the dogs scraps of sharky gossip & kissed

the dealer to take the edge off. But, you sent me packing.
Now, I think I'll fall in love with the bottle-blonde,
the one listing near the table with her thumbnail cracked
to the quick. *Sister*, I'll whisper, *a handful of clubs will never*
summon luck. Burn that pack with pepper. And quick.

Field Notes From the Republic

for Violet

1.

You girl, you're full of questions these days.
I'd tip-tap out a map but my hands shake
and I still can't read the stars. I hear William Clark
was dead-on with dead reckoning – only 40 miles off
after 8,000 miles. And me? I've been to 26 states
this year to get a bead on the Republic and all I can say is:
This country's too big. I'd go in alphabetical order
but I'd have to skip Arizona. Too planetary.

2.

The Florida pelicans you love are corseted in oil
and a boy not yet 8 vanished from a high-hilled
school near home. The glaciers are melting in Montana
and spring came a full 3 weeks early to Delaware
though you'd never have known it around here.
We had a blackberry winter and all the barges
are hauling logs up river. I heard that Andromeda
is 45 light years from earth. We'd have to find
each other with red tacks & twine.

3.

In Washington, the furrier's been chased of town
with spittle on his lips, and the Virginians are still hiding
behind their un-hired help. Violet, I miss your lightning
fast figuring of the trade-ins or trade-offs or trade -ups.
For me, compensation comes in the form of a cocktail
or a well-timed firecracker. I'm not even sure
which of Alabama's gun-metal frills to pass along.
But, let me tell you this: Always call
on the bees to mourn a mother's death.

Sweet countryman—or is that countrygirl?—
there's a sandhill crane on the golf-course
in Utah and a nosegay of Ohio hummingbirds
humming down the list: forced air & four-door
& pay-per-view. Of course, there are wrinkle-free slacks
and self-cleaning ovens in Kentucky. I am one to fret
the future but can't think past the national highway system
& garage door openers & one-pot suppers.
I do know this: invention is the mother of necessity.

5.

In West Virginia, they say the death tick sounds
like an old-fashioned clock. But I'm not so sure.
The cherry tree you climb in the yard is blowsy
but barren. Reminds me of old Clark leaning back
in his cherry velvet chair, celebrating Missouri and lording
the Indians. Sure, the late light's fine and frail but the oil's still
slicking and the boy's still missing. It takes practice to perfect a piecrust.

6.

Listen, sweet tea, the other day I saw a hobo trim
his woman's hair next to the old maple tree at home.
Brushed it book-straight with a dimestore comb
then shook the red gold cloud into the tufted morning light.
And tomorrow, love, you'll ask me again and then again—
like a flurry of bruise-colored moths set loose in the house—
Is oil still spilling into the ocean? Is that little boy still missing
his mama? Yes. The answer, my girl, is yes.

Speaking of Pyromancy or the Promise of Divination by Fire

for D.

Last evening I could not for the life of me recall
the name for sumac.   Even as its scarlet tips
wicked the sun's last hour, flamed out,
and then half-shimmered in the near-dark.
I wanted to call you out, my love, but I could not recall.
Sycamore? No. Then it was just milkweed

and lambs ear come to mind. All light and no heat.
Or maybe it's the other way around. It took till late
to recall—*ah, su-mac*—while I was lying awake,
wondering how you feel now that we're in ordinary time.
Now that we're out of the coffee shop and into the bed.
One thing leads to another. A coffee cup, a kerosene flame,

the end of the virgin queen. Don't quote me on that.
You know, my mother planted sumac near the back door.
Fingered the sticky leaves as she walked back and forth
with the wash. I don't know why. Probably for the same reason
she set down overcooked lima beans and fatback,
wore blue-beaded moccasins in the house.

When the long-short vowels of sumac came back,
I was lying there lying to myself, pretending I could not see
the blue migraine promise stalking the edges of my eyes,
of my mind, like a dream ready to resurface once you hear
the words *tack sail* or glimpse the tail of a garter snake whip
into the heat of a cracked foundation. Beginning:

tingling edges, a film of lead on the tongue.
Middle: Bunsen-burner-blind and the tip
of a fireplace poker to the scalp. End: lying
alone in the dark. I don't want to die
in West Virginia. You *can* quote me on that.
It's time now to tell you darling,

my father's brother set my grandmother on fire.
Outright. A gas can. A cigarette. Polyester pants.
All things I've avoided but I'm not sure what it says
about the gene pool. And, meanwhile my little
daughter's singing *Jackson* in the backseat:
We got married in a fever. Hotter than a pepper sprout.

We've been talking 'bout Jackson. Ever since the fire went out.
Of all people, I know you understand wayward
brothers and the songs of children. But still, there's
so much to tell. My one and only, last night a horsewoman
hummed a three-bit song with the tongue of a thrush. I know
that arsenic burns blue & honey never rots. Chevala Vargas

was Frida Kahlo's lover. She said: *I drank everything
I ever owned. That's why I left nothing over there.*
And John Wesley (recalling the psalmist): *I just set
myself on fire and folks come to watch me burn.*
And you, your own sweet self: *You're dead longer
than you're alive. A lot longer.* You have a tell, my one,

that smells of smoke. And somewhere in the sulphur-burning-
yellow of my mind, I can see forward, to that moment
where death swirls as a stinking sea mist and life is solid
as a cast iron pot. But the wind shifts. And death
is a bucket of wet sand and what's left? A whisper
in the dark—*sumac*—and smudged lipstick on a cup.

QUICKED

I wanted to begin with *once upon a time*,
with trilly notes stacked like teacups,
the sky white and open. I'd say *Yes*—

a dark and stormy night. A hero's quest.
But there's salt in my teeth and the wind
won't rest. The arc breaks and I can't stop

singing: *the ankle bone connected to the
shin bone.* Grandiosity is its own reward.
Unarmed with apron or jelly jar or ladle,

the bump and thrust, the fast-growing sod,
the urge of the urge. Oh man oh man oh man. Yes, then,

let it in.

The Half-Life of Strawberries

"Sweeter. Redder. Simply Better."
  —slogan, Oregon Strawberry Commission

The first strawberries were brought to Oregon in a covered wagon by Henderson Luelling. By 1957, there were 18,300 acres of Oregon farmland devoted to strawberries. Now, there are fewer than 2,000 acres.

"They are not good for a healthy or sick person to eat because they grow near the earth and because they also grow in putrid air."
  —Hildegard of Bingen

"Various female figures stand out for the holiness of their lives and the wealth of their teaching even in those centuries of history that we usually call the Middle Ages. Today I would like to begin to present one of them to you: St. Hildegard of Bingen, who lived in Germany in the 12th century. . . [T]his 'prophetess' . . . also speaks with great timeliness to us today, with her courageous ability to discern the signs of the times, her love for creation, her medicine, her poetry, her music, which today has been reconstructed, her love for Christ and for his Church which was suffering in that period too, wounded also in that time by the sins of both priests and lay people, and far better loved as the Body of Christ."
  —H.H. Pope Benedict XVI
   September 1, 2010

Economies

Weyerhaeuser Pulp & Paper Mill • 785 42nd Street • Springfield, Oregon.

On July 23, 1990, the United States Fish and Wildlife Service listed the Northern Spotted Owl as a threatened species, effectively ending large-scale logging in Western Oregon.

On June 13, 1966, the Supreme Court decided *Miranda v. Arizona*, creating a police script that nearly every American can recite by heart. Six days later, Wendy Willis was born.

"Clock repair makes time pass for Pendleton inmates: The men at an eastern Oregon prison remake grandfather and antique pieces into something new, giving them a purpose and a goal while incarcerated."
　　—Richard Cockle, *The Oregonian*

Genealogy

Wendy Willis' great-grandmother, Frieda Severson Toll, and her seven daughters—Edna, Ethel, Donna, Eva, Ione, Margie & Helen.

Ione's Christmas Cake as Perfected by Edna
1 ½ cup whole Brazil nuts
1 ½ cup walnut halves
1 ½ cup pitted dates
2 cups combined candied cherries and pineapple
¾ cup sifted flower
¾ cup sugar
½ tsp. baking powder
½ tsp. salt
3 eggs
1 tsp. vanilla

Grease bottom and sides of a loaf pan—preferably one of Edna's oval pans—and line bottom with parchment or waxed paper.

Put nuts & fruit in a large bowl. Sift flour, sugar, baking powder & salt over fruit & nuts. Mix well. Beat eggs & vanilla together until light & fluffy. Mix into other ingredients. Spoon into pan & bake.

Bake at 300 degrees for two hours.
Cool in pan for 10 minutes.

Wrap in a cloth moistened with brandy.

In astrology, a balsamic moon occurs when the moon is 45 degrees behind the natal sun. The balsamic moon is reputed to relate to one's commitment to destiny.

The Marriage of Flax and Wool

"Thou shalt not wear a garment of divers sorts, as of woollen and linen together."
—Deuteronomy 22:11

Quicked

A solid sourdough start is a treasure that can be passed down from generation to generation. In a large bowl, mix together two cups of warm water, a package of active dry yeast, and two cups of all purpose flour. Cover loosely and let sit for four to eight days. When the start is bubbly and smelling sour, put it in the fridge until time to use. When you take a piece to bake bread, replenish the start with equal amounts of flour and water and a pinch of sugar. Let bubble, then return to the fridge. Sourdough starts improve with age.

Paper mache volcanoes were the rage of 1970s third-grade classrooms. To produce lava: 2 tbsp. baking soda, ¼ cup warm water, ½ cup vinegar, a few drops red food coloring.

Fixed Time

"A Haberdasher, a Dyer, a Carpenter,
A Weaver and a Carpet-maker were
Among our ranks, all in the livery
Of one impressive guild-fraternity."
—*from* The Five Guildsman, Canterbury Tales

Herbert Hoover's Ghost Is the Fourteenth Guest

Herbert Hoover, the nation's 31st president, lived in Oregon from the time he was orphaned in 1885 until 1891, when he went to Stanford University in Northern California. Those six years remain the state's closest brush with siring a president.

Pear Tree, Hoover-Minthorn House, Newberg, Oregon

"What fruit therefore had I (in my vileness) in those things of which I am now ashamed? Especially in that piece of thieving, in which I loved nothing except the thievery—though that in itself was no thing and I only the more wretched for it. "
—St. Augustine, *The Confessions of St. Augustine*, Book II, Chapter VIII

Hoover: it's proved a fine verb.

Oblation

In a pinch, you can make a Frangelico coconut cake with a yellow cake mix, a quarter cup of Frangelico, and a half teaspoon of almond extract. Follow the instructions on the box, adding the Frangelico and almond extract. Then, frost with whipped cream and top with coconut flakes.

"'Take and eat; this is my body.' Then he took a cup, gave thanks, and gave it to them, saying, 'Drink from it, all of you, for this is my blood of the covenant, which will be shed on behalf of many for the forgiveness of sins.'"
—Matthew 26:26-28

Fruitcake Weather

Forsyth County Courthouse, Winston-Salem, North Carolina: Latitude: 36.10 N, Longitude: 80.26 W.

A House Divided

April 9th, 1865.

General: Your note of yesterday is received. I have not authority to treat on the subject of peace. The meeting proposed for 10 A.M. to-day could lead to no good. I will state, however, that I am equally desirous for peace with yourself, and the whole North entertains the same feeling. The terms upon which peace can be had are well understood. By the South laying down their arms, they would hasten that most desirable event, save thousands of human lives, and hundreds of millions of property not yet destroyed. Seriously hoping that all our difficulties may be settled without the loss of another life, I subscribe myself, etc.,
　　　　　—U.S. Grant, Lieutenant-General

At 4:00 p.m., on April 9, 1865, General Robert E. Lee of the Army of the Confederacy, surrendered to General Ulysses S. Grant, commanding general for the United States at Appomattox Courthouse, Virginia. Wilmer McLean owned both the farm where the war began in the First Battle of Bull Run and the house in Appomattox Courthouse, where Lee surrendered. The war, as they say, began in McLean's front yard and ended in his parlor.

To make wine jelly, mix a box of fruit pectin and three-quarters of a cup of water. Bring it to a full boil and let it roll for one minute, stirring constantly. Reduce to medium and add three cups of tart wine and four cups of sugar. Cook until sugar is dissolved, then remove from heat and remove foam with a spoon. Ladle into sterilized jars and seal with bands and lids. Invert the jars for five minutes, then cool and shelve. Serve with cream cheese and toast.

Easter Eggs for Ruby

Gloucester Style-Elver Cake
Fill a pillow case with elvers (young eels). Wash off the slimy mucous and squeeze out the moisture. In a frying pan, fry two slices of bacon until crispy. Remove the bacon from the pan and add the elvers. Cook until opaque. Slightly beat two eggs and add to the pan. Add onion juice and herbs to taste. Pour over bacon and press into a dish. Cool until hard set.
 —adapted from Tom Parker Bowles, *A Year of Eating Dangerously: A Global Adventure in Search of Culinary Extremes.* (2008)

To coppice an ash or any other tree, cut it near ground level, leaving enough stem to allow new growth. If properly coppiced, a tree can live for hundreds of years.

Violet's Kite

"You have your whole life to wear a black dress."
 —Edna Leathers

In converting dry measures, a cup of sugar is 7.055 ounces. A cup of flour is 4.409 ounces.

On Easter Sunday 2010, high tide was at 4:12 a.m. It was followed by an extreme low tide at 10:08 a.m.

Dear Dumpling

"Extract the Juice of 20 pounds of well ripend Morrella Cherrys. Add to this 10 quarts of Old French brandy and sweeten it with White Sugar to your taste—To 5 Gallons of this mixture add one ounce of Spice Such as Cinnamon, Cloves and Nutmegs of each an Equal quantity Slightly bruis'd and a pint and half of Cherry kernels that have been gently broken in a mortar—After the liquor has fermented let it Stand Close-Stoped for a month or Six weeks—then bottle it remembering to put a lump of Loaf Sugar into each bottle."
 —Martha Washington, Recipe for Cherry Bounce

When a hen gets broody, candle her eggs by shining a bright light through them. You will see a web of veins if a chick is developing. Otherwise, it's just a yolk.

House Finch Returns To Chastise the Household
for Its Late Winter Lassitude

force majeure: 1) unforeseeable circumstances that prevent someone from fulfilling a contract; 2) irresistible compulsion or superior strength.

planquer: 1) to hide away; 2) a hideaway.

Seven Ways To Conjure the Luck of the Saltwater Sturgeon

Fred Willis, Russell Maine & two sturgeons in North Bend, Oregon

How It Came To Be That the Rook Took the Queen

Pythagorean Theorem:

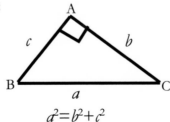

$$a^2 = b^2 + c^2$$

78

The chess rook can move any number of squares—but only in straight lines, up and down, or side to side.

Thinking About Mary Baird Bryan Waiting for Her Husband To Return From the Oregon State Fair While I Wait for My Own New Husband To Come Home and the Republicans To Take Over the House of Representatives

In November 1888, Mary Baird Bryan was admitted to the practice of law in Nebraska. In January 1994, Wendy Willis was admitted to the Oregon State Bar.

In 1893, William Jennings Bryan visited the Oregon State Fair, making a speech about the importance of buying local products. He is rumored to have purchased two Salem-made blankets.

Until recent years, it was a misdemeanor in Oregon to exhibit a person in a trance, whether the cause was hypnotism or mesmerism.
    —*Oregon Revised Statutes 167.870. (historical)*

Quick-Knit Baby Booties
Using size five needles and sport weight yarn,
Cast on 29 stitches
Knit 10 rows in garter stitch
To decrease
K12, K2tog, K1, K2tog, K12
P11, P2tog, P1, P2tog, P11
Continue decrease pattern until 19 are stitches left.

Ribbed Cuff:
K1 P1 across each row for 4 rows. Double the rows for a fold down cuff.
Bind off loosely.
Sew back and sole of bootie.

The Second Half-Life of Strawberries

Anne Boleyn, second wife of Henry VIII and mother of Elizabeth I, was said to have had a third nipple and six fingers on her right hand, adding to the rumor that she was a witch who had beguiled King Henry into abandoning the Catholic Church and annulling his marriage to Queen Catherine of Aragon. She was beheaded on May 19, 1536. Oddly, also on May 19, but in the year 1499, Catherine of Aragon had married Henry's older brother, Arthur, Prince of Wales. Unfortunately for all, Arthur died of the sweating sickness on April 2, 1502.

A mole = 6.022×10^{23}, the number of molecules in 22.41 liters of gas. In 1811, Amedeo Avogadro first proposed that the volume of gas is proportional to the number of molecules, regardless of the gas. In his honor, the mole is also known as Avogadro's Number.

St. John's Day is June 24.

And It Appears That—Once Again—All the Blues Are on Hand

Vincent Van Gogh's *Portrait of Postman Roulin*—the one with the blue wall—was passed from Theo Van Gogh to Johanna Van Gogh-Bonger to Gallery Paul Cassiser to J. Freudenberg to Arnold Sigmann to Edsel and Eleonor Ford to Mrs. Walter Ford to—in the end—the Detroit Institute of Art, where you can visit it today.

Enchanté. Enchanted.
Désolé. Sorry.
Mal de mer. Sea sickness.
Fou Rou. Crazy Red.
Mal de tête. Headache.
Sacré Bleu! Sacred blue (referring to Mary, mother of Jesus).
Beni soit l'oubli. Blessed is the forgotten.
Beni soit le bleu. Blessed is the blue.

Writing Home From Alabama on the Anniversary of Asking *What Is It That Attracts You Personally to the Crow?* Then Passing Ted Hughes From Hand to Hand in All His Bloodiness

"And mouths cried 'Mamma'
From sudden traps of calculus,
Theorems wrenched men in two,
Shock-severed eyes watched blood
Squandering as if from a drainpipe…"
　　　　—Ted Hughes, "Crow's Account of the Battle," *Crow*

Q: "What is it, Major Lawrence, that attracts you, personally, to the desert?"
A: "It's clean."
　　　　—Lawrence of Arabia

"The folks in Mississippi are saying, 'Thank God for Texas.'"
　　　　—Kinky Friedman

St. Eulalia is the patron saint of widows and torture victims. Her feast day is December 10.

The civil war battle ship the U.S.S. Tecumseh was launched from Jersey City, New Jersey, on September 12, 1863. It was sunk in the Battle of Mobile Bay on August 5, 1864.

Field Notes From the Republic

A blackberry winter is a cold May when the blackberries are in bloom.

After the Expedition, William Clark became the Governor of the Missouri Territory and the Superintendent of Indian Affairs.

On June 14, 2010, eight-year-old Kyron Horman disappeared from his grade school in Southwest Portland. He has never been found.

Tips to perfect a piecrust:
1. Before making the dough, put everything in the refrigerator, even the flour.
2. Unfortunately, lard makes the most tender crust, with shortening a near second. If you must, use half shortening and half butter.
3. Use a pastry blender or two knives to cut the fat into the flour. Handle as little as possible.
4. All liquids should be ice-cold.
5. Blend liquid in just until the dough begins to hold together. Overworking toughens the dough.

Speaking of Pyromancy or the Promise of Divination by Fire

Sumac

The Bunsen burner was invented by German chemist, Robert Wilhelm Bunsen, in 1855.

Chevala Vargas is Costa-Rican born singer who—in her youth—smoked cigars, carried a gun, and made *rancheras* music famous to international audiences.

John Wesley was the 18th Century father of the Methodist movement. He was known for his open-air preaching, occasionally using his father's tombstone as a pulpit.

A Note From the Poet

Tremendous gratitude to many fellow travelers: To all the sisters, mothers, grandmothers, and daughters in my life, especially my own rock-solid mother, Tonya Willis, and darling sister, Amy Willis Stranieri. To Greg Glazner, Lia Purpura, and David Keplinger for being generous readers. To Tom Lombardo for being a fierce and open-hearted editor and to Kevin Watson for making Press 53 what it is. To my dad, Fred Willis, for his wonderful photographs. To Patty Maher for her incredible cover photo. To Ruby and Violet for understanding why their mama is hunkered down in the studio instead of doing the laundry and for being the reason. And, to David for always believing and for coming closer yet.

WENDY WILLIS splits her time between her roles as mother, poet, and advocate for democracy. She is the Executive Director of the Policy Consensus Initiative, a national non-profit organization housed at Oregon State University, devoted to improving democratic governance. In addition to publishing poetry and essays in a variety of national and regional journals and serving as an adjunct fellow in poetry at the Attic Institute, Willis has served as a federal public defender and as the law clerk to Chief Justice Wallace P. Carson, Jr. of the Oregon Supreme Court. She graduated *magna cum laude* from Georgetown Law Center and holds a B.A. in political science from Willamette University. She lives in Portland, Oregon, with her husband, his son and her two young daughters.

Cover artist **Patty Maher** is a self-taught photographer based in Caledon, Ontario, and derives her inspiration from the beautiful countryside in which she lives. In this environment she is moved to tell stories through the art of portraiture—stories that explore the boundaries between real life and the otherworldly, the surreal and the fantastic. Patty's work has been featured in numerous online and print publications.

Patty says of her process: "When I take self portraits, I usually get inspired by a basic idea: it could be a prop or a location that inspires me, or a visual idea or series of words that pop into my head and just won't leave. The process of taking the photos itself is quite free flowing and I just go with what occurs to me when I'm on location. It is very meditative and I find that no matter what kind of day I've had I emerge from this process feeling calm and centered. Sometimes I am able to capture what I had in mind and sometimes I end up with something entirely different—but I'm always looking for the photo that has some kind of magic inside it, whether it is a specific quality of light, a slight movement or tweak of a posture that simply makes that photo stand out from the rest. It's something that can't be recreated twice. For me, photography is the pursuit of capturing that magic."

To see more of Patty's work, visit www.flickr.com/photos/closetartist/

CPSIA information can be obtained at www.ICGtesting.com
Printed in the USA
BVOW081501090912

299890BV00002B/16/P